DKfindout!
Universe

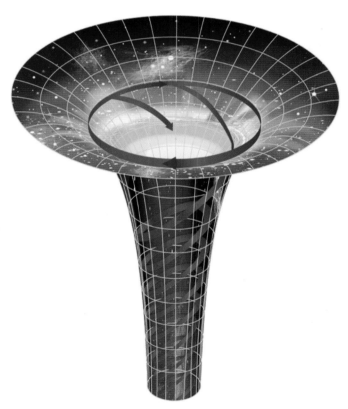

Author: Giles Sparrow
Consultant: Jerry Stone

Penguin Random House

Senior editor Carrie Love
Project art editor Lucy Sims
Project editor Ishani Nandi
Editor Anwesha Dutta
Assistant editor Shambhavi Thatte
Art editors Kartik Gera, Shipra Jain
Managing editors Laura Gilbert, Alka Thakur Hazarika
Managing art editors Diane Peyton Jones,
Romi Chakraborty
Jacket designer Suzena Sengupta
Jacket coordinator Francesca Young
DTP designers Rajesh Singh Adhikari, Pawan Kumar
Picture researcher Sakshi Saluja
CTS manager Balwant Singh
Pre-producer Rob Dunn
Senior producer Isabell Schart
Creative director Helen Senior
Publishing director Sarah Larter
Educational consultant Jacqueline Harris

First published in Great Britain in 2018 by
Dorling Kindersley Limited
80 Strand, London, WC2R 0RL

Copyright © 2018 Dorling Kindersley Limited
A Penguin Random House Company
10 9 8 7 6 5 4 3 2 1
001–308808–Sep/2018

A CIP catalogue record for this book
is available from the British Library.
ISBN: 978-0-2413-2287-1

Printed and bound in China

A WORLD OF IDEAS:
SEE ALL THERE IS TO KNOW

www.dk.com

Contents

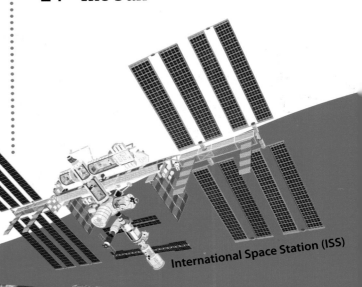

International Space Station (ISS)

Replica of Galileo's telescope

St

What to spot

There are lots of excit...
a stargazer and look...
and our Moon. They'...

Meteo...

Watch out for meteo...
Earth is passing throu...
and a meteor shower is...

...planets

...ions at night
...hat are easy
...as Venus.

love your library

...es

Buckinghamshire ...line 24/7

Search, renew or rese...raries

www.buckscc.go...

...al line

24 hour r...0035

0303...

...uiries

...96 382415

follow us **twitter**

@Bucks_Libraries

ISS

The International Space Station can
be seen from the Earth. Check out
NASA's website for timings.

The Moon

During one month, draw the shape
of the Moon you see each night.
...e changes.

Things to find out:

Moon rock

Inside the planet Mars

Space Shuttle Discovery

United States

Discovery

Hockey Stick Galaxy

Our place in space

Our Universe is enormous – in fact it's everything there is. Long ago, people used to think that Earth was the centre of everything, but now we understand that our planet is just one tiny speck in space.

Where do we fit in?

The scale of the Universe is so huge that we can't really imagine it all in one go. The best way of thinking about it is to see how things from our everyday lives fit into it.

THE SOLAR SYSTEM

Our Solar System is mostly empty space – even our Moon is 30 Earth diameters away. Earth is 150 million km (93 million miles) from the Sun, but distant comets can orbit up to a light year away.

OUR PLANET

The Earth is 12,742 km (7,918 miles) across – it would take an average person about 20 million steps to walk around the equator.

CITIES

Medium-sized cities are usually 10–20 km (6–12 miles) across – it might take a few hours to cross them by foot.

PEOPLE

Most people are between 1–2 m (3–6$^1/_2$ ft) tall – walking at average speed, we cover about 5 km (3 miles) in an hour.

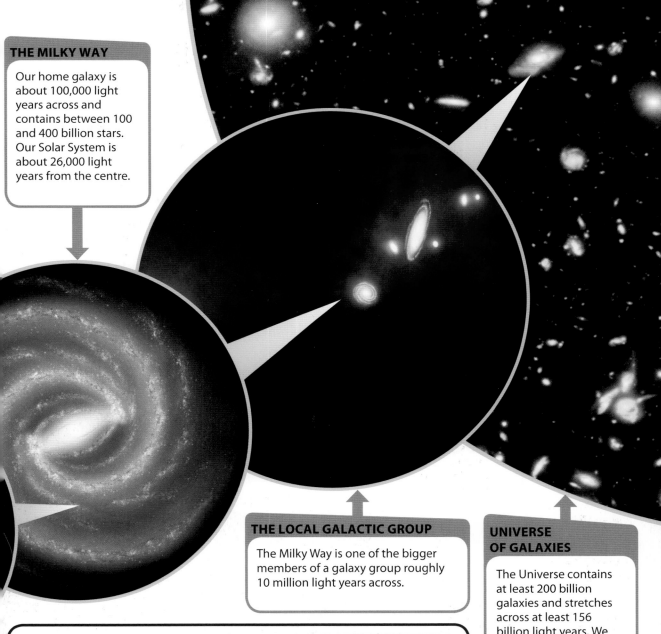

THE MILKY WAY

Our home galaxy is about 100,000 light years across and contains between 100 and 400 billion stars. Our Solar System is about 26,000 light years from the centre.

THE LOCAL GALACTIC GROUP

The Milky Way is one of the bigger members of a galaxy group roughly 10 million light years across.

UNIVERSE OF GALAXIES

The Universe contains at least 200 billion galaxies and stretches across at least 156 billion light years. We can see objects up to 92 billion light years away.

What is a light year?

Astronomers measure huge cosmic distances in terms of light years, the distance that light (the fastest thing in the Universe), travels in one year. One light year is about 9.5 trillion km or 5.9 trillion miles.

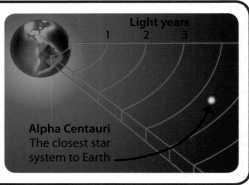

Light years

1   2   3   4

Alpha Centauri
The closest star system to Earth

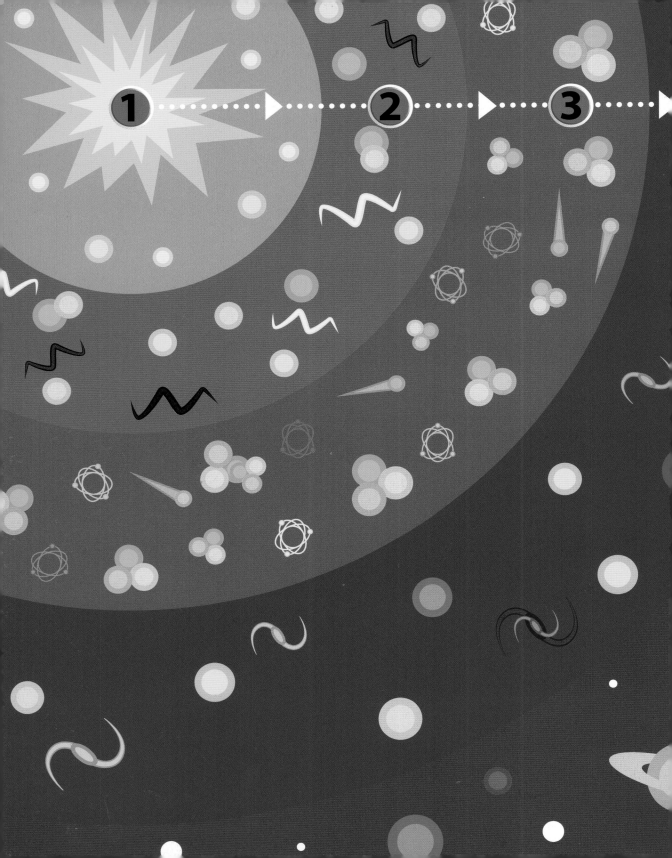

The Universe is still expanding from the Big Bang – in fact, it's growing faster than ever.

4 **5**

The Big Bang

The Universe was born in an explosion called the Big Bang, 13.8 billion years ago. The Big Bang created all the matter in the Universe. Matter is the stuff that everything is made of. It took a long time for that matter to clump together into larger objects, such as planets, moons, and stars.

Stars

Stars are huge balls of gas that release heat and light. They are often found in pairs or clusters.

Space objects

The Universe contains objects, from asteroids, planets like Earth, to stars, many far bigger than our Sun, and enormous galaxies! Then there are the objects that humans have sent into space, including satellites and spacecraft.

Planets

There are different types of planet that orbit the stars; rocky planets like the Earth, gas planets like Jupiter, and dwarf planets like Pluto. The planet shown here is Venus.

Galaxies

Galaxies are the largest objects in the Universe. They are made up of many millions of stars, along with gas and dust.

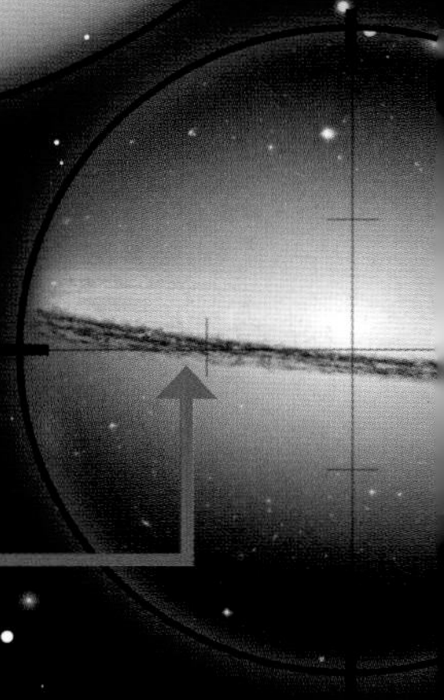

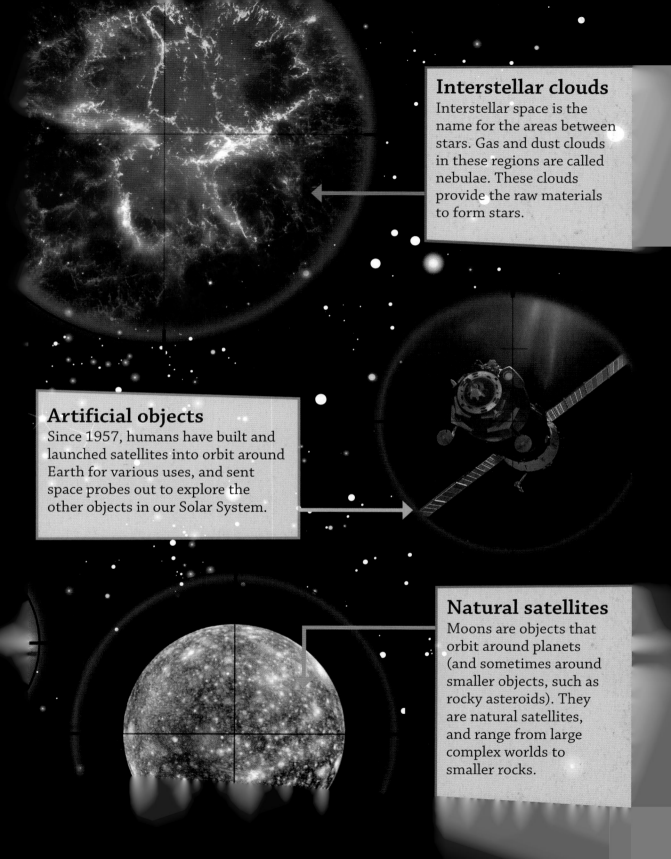

Interstellar clouds

Interstellar space is the name for the areas between stars. Gas and dust clouds in these regions are called nebulae. These clouds provide the raw materials to form stars.

Artificial objects

Since 1957, humans have built and launched satellites into orbit around Earth for various uses, and sent space probes out to explore the other objects in our Solar System.

Natural satellites

Moons are objects that orbit around planets (and sometimes around smaller objects, such as rocky asteroids). They are natural satellites, and range from large complex worlds to smaller rocks.

Life of a star

Stars live and die at different speeds depending on how much fuel they have to burn. Massive stars shine more fiercely but live much shorter lives than smaller ones. They also die in different ways.

Red giant
After a few billion years, a small star like the Sun goes through changes that allow it to keep shining. It gets much brighter, swells in size, and turns red.

Protostar
A star is born from a collapsing cloud of gas and dust. It warms up as the gas molecules collide, until eventually it begins to shine.

Main-sequence star
A star's "main sequence" stage is the main part of its life. During this stage it burns through the fuel supply in its hot core, and shines steadily.

Red supergiant
The biggest, brightest stars run out of fuel in just a few million years. They swell in size to become supergiants.

Planetary nebula
Eventually, a red giant becomes unstable and puffs off its outer layers into a glowing gas bubble called a planetary nebulae.

White dwarf
The Earth-sized core of the red giant survives. It cannot make any more energy, but still shines because its surface is extremely hot.

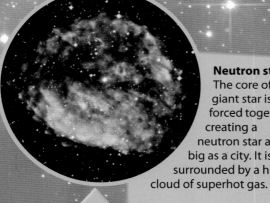

Neutron star
The core of a giant star is forced together, creating a neutron star as big as a city. It is surrounded by a huge cloud of superhot gas.

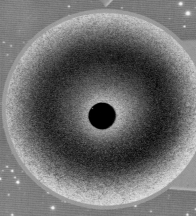

Black dwarf
Over many billions of years, a white dwarf slowly cools down until it can become a thick, dark, black dwarf.

Supernova
When a supergiant runs out of fuel, it dies in a huge explosion called a supernova that can outshine a galaxy of normal stars.

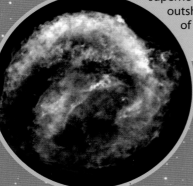

Black hole
A black hole is a point in space that sucks in anything that comes close to it. Stars with very heavy cores (centres) collapse to create black holes.

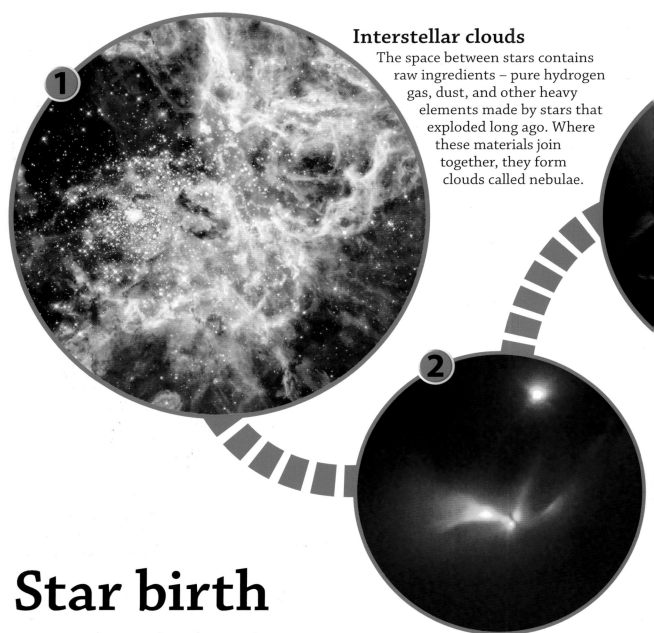

Interstellar clouds

The space between stars contains raw ingredients – pure hydrogen gas, dust, and other heavy elements made by stars that exploded long ago. Where these materials join together, they form clouds called nebulae.

Star birth

Stars are born when huge clouds of gas and dust floating in space are condensed by gravity, or are disturbed by the gravity of another star passing nearby, or the shockwave from a supernova explosion. Hundreds or thousands of stars may be born from a single cloud.

Protostar

As a nebula collapses, it separates into protostars – knots of gas that will each form one or more stars. A protostar's gravity pulls in material from its surroundings.

Spinning disc

3 As the protostar draws matter inwards, it flattens out into a disc with a bulging centre. It spins quickly and gets hotter and hotter as it pulls in more material, spitting out extra matter in jets.

4

New star

Eventually the gas at the centre of the disc gets hot and thick enough for nuclear reactions to begin, turning it into a shining star.

5

Planets form

Material left in the disc around the star can now start to form a system of planets, which can include both rocky planets and those made mostly of gas. Gas planets are generally much bigger than rocky planets, but either type can be found close to a star or further away.

Types of stars

The billions of stars in the sky vary hugely in colour, size, and brightness. Some of these differences are because stars are born with varying weights, and some because they are at different stages in their life cycle.

Colour range

A star's colour depends on how hot it is. A star's temperature is measured in degrees Kelvin (K). Zero degrees Kelvin is -273 °C (-458 °F).

Hottest

> 30,000 K

10,000–30,000 K

Blue giant
Stars with several times the Sun's mass shine a hundred times brighter, so their super-hot surfaces appear blue.

Blue supergiant
These stars weigh tens of times more than the Sun and shine a hundred-thousand times more brightly.

The Sun
The Sun is an average star with a yellow surface. It will shine steadily for billions of years before turning into a red giant.

Dwarf stars

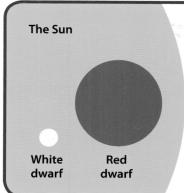

The Sun

White dwarf

Red dwarf

Red dwarfs are normal stars that are much cooler, fainter and smaller than the Sun. Red dwarfs are the most common type of star in the Milky Way. White dwarfs are as big as planets. They are the burnt-out cores of stars.

Coldest

| 5,200 – 6,000 K | 3,700 – 5,200 K | 3,000 – 4,000 K | 2,400 – 3,700 K |

Orange giant

Stars with less mass than the Sun do not brighten or swell so much near the end of their lives.

Red giant

Near the end of their lives, stars like the Sun briefly shine as brilliant, huge but cool red giants.

Red supergiant

These are the biggest stars of all, with puffy atmospheres that can be larger than Jupiter's orbit around the Sun.

Multiple stars

Stars are born in large groups out of gas clouds that fall apart. Some drift away to become single stars like the Sun, but most spend their whole lives in pairs, triplets or bigger groups.

This multiple star system has two binary pairs in orbit around each other.

Binary stars

Astronomers call a pair of stars in orbit around each other a "binary system". The time it takes stars in a binary system to circle each other can vary from a few hours to thousands of years.

Merging stars

Two stars in a binary pair may not have the same mass, or amount of matter. If this is the case, they will age at different rates. This can allow one star to steal material from the other.

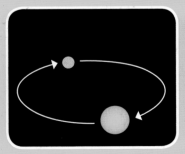

1. Orbiting stars
In this binary pair, one star is a white dwarf and the other is about to become a red giant.

2. Matter transfer
The white dwarf star steals gas from the outer layers of the star that has become a red giant.

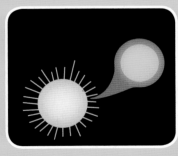

3. White dwarf explodes
The shell of hot gas around the white dwarf burns away in an explosion called a nova.

Clusters

Groups of stars can be formed from the same nebula. This can result in young "open clusters," or groups of stars, that contain less than 100 members, such as the Pleiades star cluster. Pleiades is also called Seven Sisters.

Seven bright stars in Pleiades are visible without using a telescope.

Black holes

A black hole is an area of space that has an incredibly strong gravity. It sometimes forms when a star collapses and dies, when huge clouds of gas join together in new galaxies, or when stars collide. If something comes too close to a black hole, it will fall in and never escape!

①

FACT FILE

» **1. Singularity** The centre of a black hole is called the "singularity". At this point, gravity becomes limitless and the normal laws of science no longer apply.

» **2. Event horizon** This boundary marks the space where even light cannot escape the black hole's gravity. This is why the black hole appears completely black.

» **3. Ergosphere** This is the area of a black hole where objects have their last chance to escape, depending on the distance between the object and the event horizon.

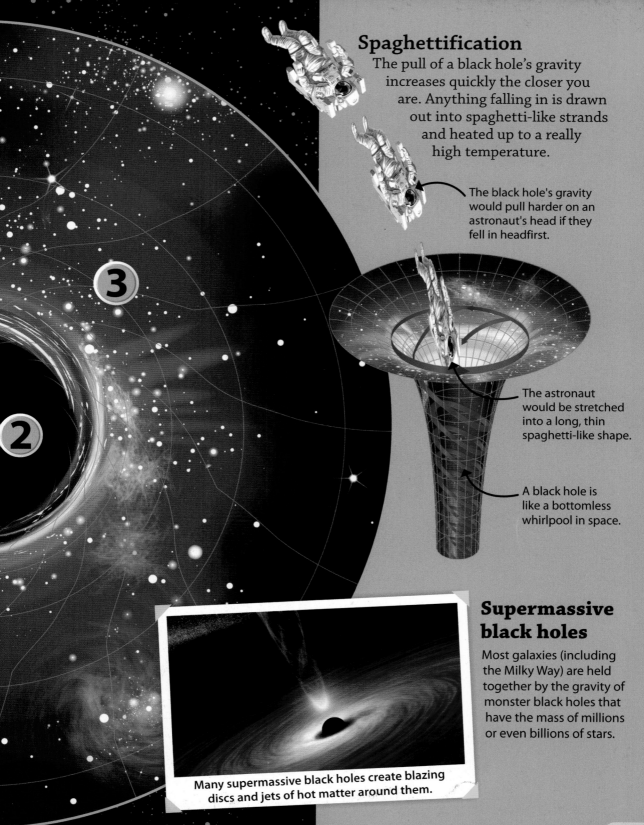

Spaghettification

The pull of a black hole's gravity increases quickly the closer you are. Anything falling in is drawn out into spaghetti-like strands and heated up to a really high temperature.

The black hole's gravity would pull harder on an astronaut's head if they fell in headfirst.

The astronaut would be stretched into a long, thin spaghetti-like shape.

A black hole is like a bottomless whirlpool in space.

Supermassive black holes

Most galaxies (including the Milky Way) are held together by the gravity of monster black holes that have the mass of millions or even billions of stars.

Many supermassive black holes create blazing discs and jets of hot matter around them.

Galaxies

A galaxy is a collection of stars, gas, and dust held together by the pulling force of gravity. Each galaxy has many millions or even billions of stars, moving together in space. There are three main galaxy shapes: elliptical, spiral, and irregular, with other sub-types.

Spiral galaxy

A lot of galaxies look like whirlpools. They have a large, very bright ball of stars in their centre, with arms of stars, gas, and dust spiralling away from it.

Messier 81

NGC 1300

Barred spiral galaxy

In this shape, a central ball is crossed by a bright bar of stars. The spiral arms begin at each end of this bar. The NGC 1300 is a barred spiral galaxy in the constellation Eridanus. Our own galaxy, the Milky Way, is a barred spiral with the Sun in one of its spiral arms.

NGC 5010

Lenticular galaxy

This type of galaxy has a central bulge of stars with no spiral arms. Its shape looks like a lens, a curved piece of glass used in a camera. Astronomers think that lenticular galaxies form after galaxies collide.

COLLIDING GALAXIES

Galaxies sometimes collide with each other over millions of years. NGC 4656 collided with NGC 4631 also known as The Whale Galaxy, and NGC 462, a small elliptical galaxy.

NGC 4656, also called Hockey Stick Galaxy

Irregular galaxy

This type of galaxy is shapeless, and mostly made up of gas and dust where new stars are forming. This dwarf galaxy in the constellation Sagittarius only has about 10 million stars.

Messier 87

Elliptical galaxy

This type has the shape of an ellipse (oval). The stars are very old and the galaxy doesn't contain much gas or dust. Supergiant ellipticals such as Messier 87 in the constellation Virgo are the largest galaxies of all.

NGC 6822

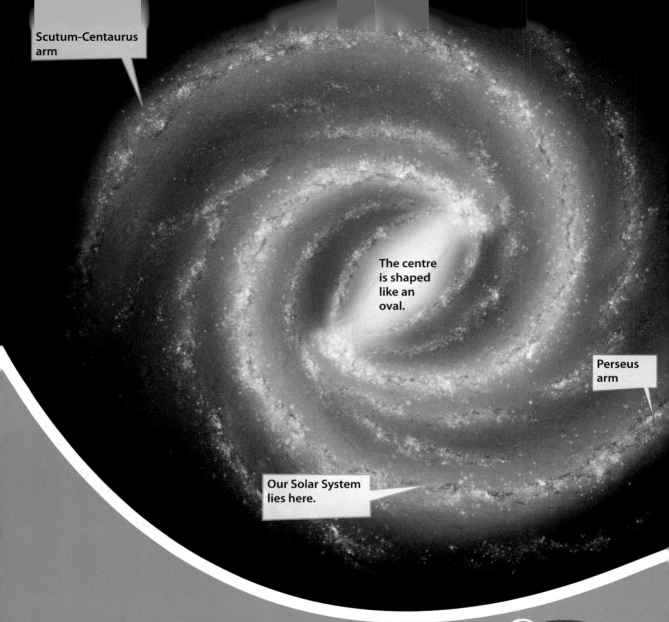

Scutum-Centaurus arm

The centre is shaped like an oval.

Perseus arm

Our Solar System lies here.

Milky Way

The Milky Way is our home galaxy. It is an enormous spiral galaxy, containing billions of stars. These are grouped together in "arms", which spiral out from the centre. Our Solar System sits inside one of the arms.

! WOW!

The Sun takes **240 million** years to make **one orbit** around the Milky Way.

Bright young stars mark out spiral

Centre of the Milky Way

From side-on, the Milky Way looks like a flattened disc with a bulge at the centre. It has lots of stars in the space around the disc.

Shape

The Milky Way is a barred spiral galaxy. An oval bulge packed with red and yellow stars is surrounded by a disc, whose brightest blue and white stars make a pattern that looks like a spiral.

The centre of the Milky Way is crowded with stars, all orbiting around an enormous black hole.

Galileo Galilei

When Italian astronomer Galileo Galilei pointed his first telescope at the pale band of the Milky Way in 1609, he discovered it was made from countless stars.

Galileo Galilei

Replica of Galileo's telescope

The Sun

The Sun is the nearest star to the Earth and lies at the centre of our Solar System. It is a huge ball of gas. The Sun produces heat and light. Without it, our planet would be lifeless. It takes the Sun's light about eight minutes to reach the Earth!

Solar gases

The Sun is mostly made of hydrogen, the lightest gas of all. At the Sun's centre, hydrogen transforms into helium, releasing energy.

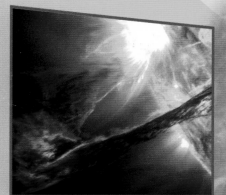

Solar flares

The Sun sometimes releases huge bursts of energy that send clouds of gas shooting across the Solar System at high speed.

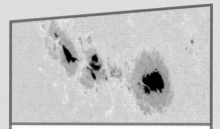

Sun spots

These shifting patches on the Sun's surface mark places where the temperature is lower than the surrounding areas.

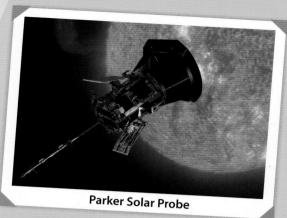

Parker Solar Probe

Exploring the Sun

Robotic probes that study the Sun must be heavily shielded from its rays. This spacecraft, built to fly into the outer part of the solar atmosphere, will face temperatures of more than 1,370 °C (2,500 °F).

Scorching surface

The Sun's surface is a layer where its gases are so thick that we can't see through them. Here, temperatures are around 5,500 °C (9,900 °F).

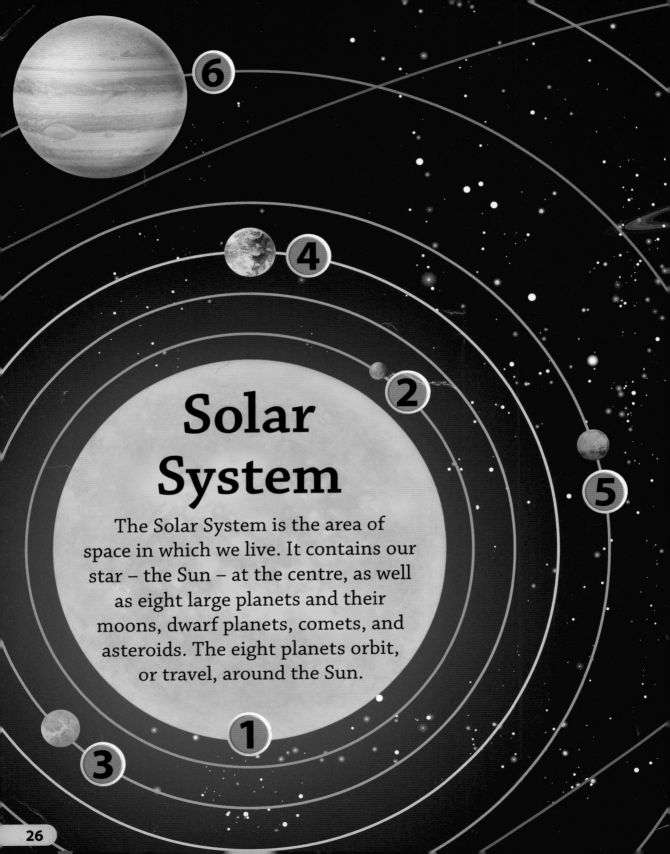

Solar System

The Solar System is the area of space in which we live. It contains our star – the Sun – at the centre, as well as eight large planets and their moons, dwarf planets, comets, and asteroids. The eight planets orbit, or travel, around the Sun.

» 1: The Sun
The Sun provides light that reflects off other Solar System objects, which is how we can see them.

» 2: Mercury
This scorching-hot, innermost planet takes just 88 days to race around the Sun.

» 3: Venus
This planet orbits the Sun in 225 days. Its volcanic surface is hidden by a thick atmosphere.

» 4: Earth
Our own planet takes 365 days to orbit the Sun. This is why our year is 365 days long.

» 5: Mars
Mars takes 687 days to orbit the Sun. A day on Mars is half an hour longer than a day on Earth.

» 6: Jupiter
Jupiter is the largest planet of all. It spins in less than 10 hours and takes almost 12 years to go around the Sun.

» 7: Saturn
This planet is the most distant one we can see without using a telescope. It takes 29.5 years to orbit the Sun.

» 8: Uranus
This cold world has an 84-year orbit. Unlike the other planets, it lies on its side.

» 9: Neptune
This outermost, major planet takes 165 years to complete a single orbit around the Sun.

» 10: Pluto
The 248-year orbit of this icy "dwarf planet" brings it closer than Neptune when it is nearest to the Sun.

» 11: Comet
Icy objects from the edge of the Solar System heat up and become active as they come close to the Sun.

Beyond Neptune

Beyond the orbit of Neptune, countless small, icy objects orbit at the edge of the Solar System. They range from dwarf planets such as Pluto to distant comets forming a shell around the Sun.

Oort Cloud
The Solar System is surrounded by a ball-like shell of comets called the Oort Cloud.

Contains comets
Trillions of comets with a total mass of about five Earths sit in the Oort cloud.

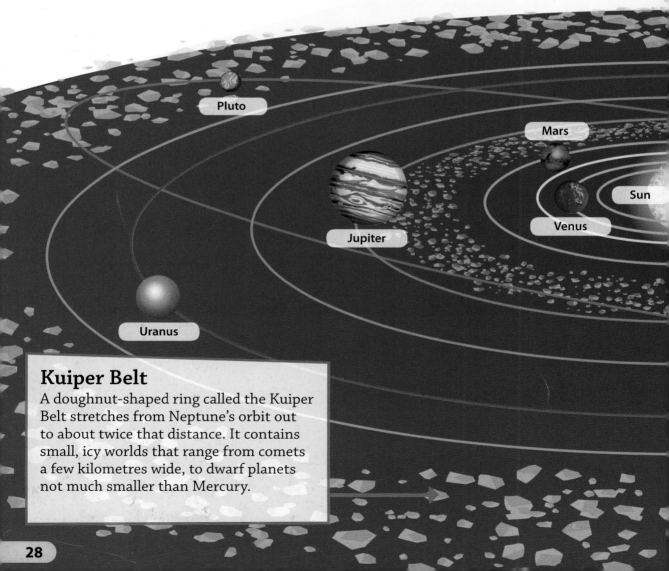

Pluto

Mars

Jupiter

Sun

Venus

Uranus

Kuiper Belt
A doughnut-shaped ring called the Kuiper Belt stretches from Neptune's orbit out to about twice that distance. It contains small, icy worlds that range from comets a few kilometres wide, to dwarf planets not much smaller than Mercury.

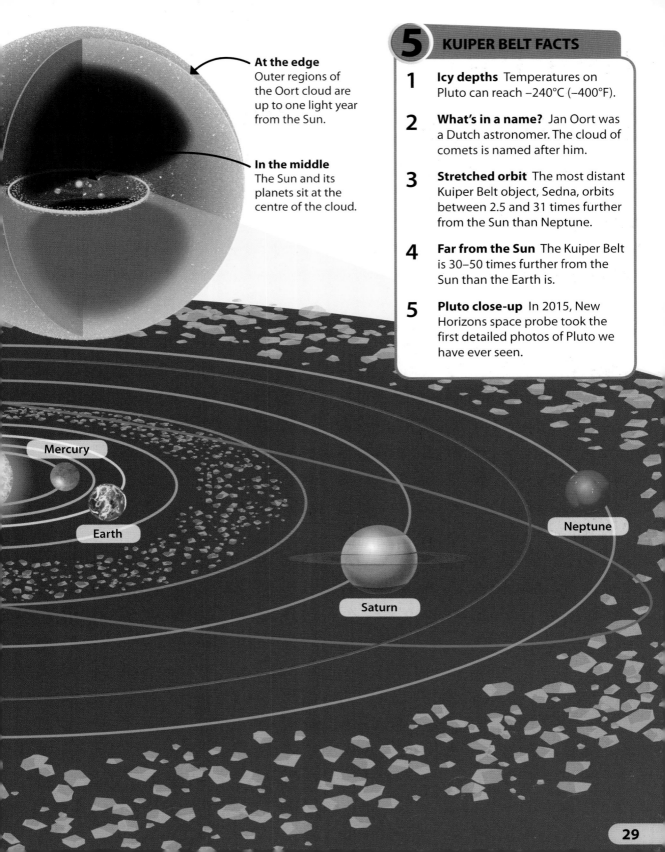

At the edge
Outer regions of the Oort cloud are up to one light year from the Sun.

In the middle
The Sun and its planets sit at the centre of the cloud.

Mercury

Earth

Saturn

Neptune

Rocky planets

The planets of the inner Solar System are all very different. Earth is the largest, followed by Venus which is nearly the same size. Mars is just over half of the Earth's size, and Mercury is even smaller.

Mercury

Mercury has an extremely hot, dry, and dusty surface. There is hardly any atmosphere to protect its surface from the strong heat of the Sun.

Mercury's surface is shaped by impacts from asteroids, comets, and meteroids.

Mercury has a large iron core.

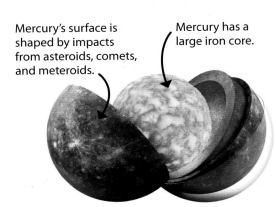

FACT FILE

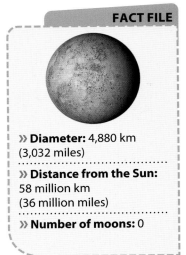

» **Diameter:** 4,880 km (3,032 miles)

» **Distance from the Sun:** 58 million km (36 million miles)

» **Number of moons:** 0

Venus

Venus is the hottest planet in the Solar System. Its volcanic, rocky surface is a scorching 482 °C (900 °F).

Volcanic eruptions occasionally flood the entire surface with lava.

Thick atmosphere can crush, boil, and burn any space probe that lands.

FACT FILE

» **Diameter:** 12,104 km (7,520 miles)

» **Distance from the Sun:** 108.2 million km (67 million miles)

» **Number of moons:** 0

Earth

The Earth is unique as it's the only planet known to be home to animal and plant life as we know it. The Earth's surface is covered with one-third land and two-thirds water.

Oceans, seas, rivers, and lakes are on the Earth's surface.

» **Diameter:** 12,742 km (7,900 miles)

» **Distance from the Sun:** 150 million km (93 million miles)

» **Number of moons:** 1

Outer crust split into slow-moving rocky plates.

Molten core of iron and nickel with a solid centre.

Atmosphere keeps temperatures even and allows life to thrive.

Mars

Mars is cold and dry, but it's the planet that is most similar to Earth. There is evidence to suggest that water once flowed across its surface. Mars may even be a home to living things.

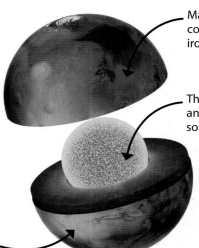

Martian crust is covered in red, iron-rich sand.

The core is small and is likely to be solid iron.

Mars has the Solar System's deepest canyons and highest mountains.

» **Diameter:** 6,779 km (4,211 miles)

» **Distance from the Sun:** 228 million km (141 million miles)

» **Number of moons:** 2

Gas giants

The huge planets of the outer Solar System are gas giants or ice giants. They are much larger than Earth, but are mostly made up of lightweight gases that turn to liquid or slushy ice deep inside. A gas giant's small core is solid and is made of rock.

Jupiter

The biggest planet of all, Jupiter is wrapped in colourful clouds, including a huge storm large enough to swallow the Earth!

Inner layer of metallic hydrogen.

Jupiter only takes 10 hours to rotate. This fast spinning makes its clouds stretch into bands.

Experts think that Jupiter's core is a ball of molten rock six times hotter than the surface of the Sun.

Outer layer of liquid hydrogen and helium.

FACT FILE

» **Diameter:** 142,984 km (88,765 miles)

» **Distance from the Sun:** 778.6 million km (483 million miles)

» **Number of moons:** 69

Saturn

Saturn has a calmer atmosphere than Jupiter because it is colder and further from the Sun. It is famous for its beautiful rings.

Cold atmosphere including clouds of ammonia crystals.

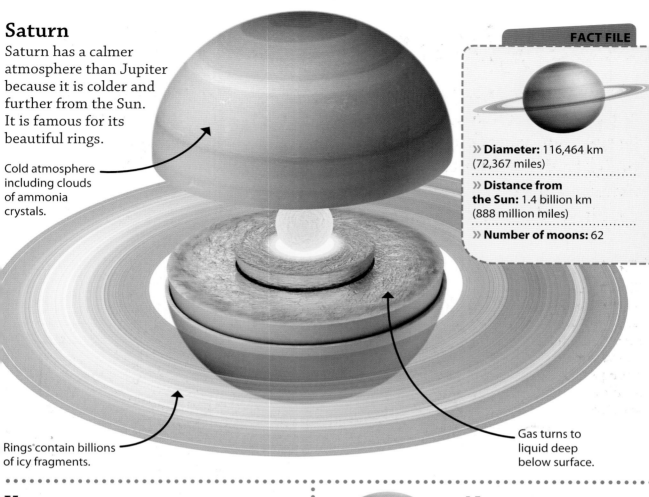

FACT FILE

» **Diameter:** 116,464 km (72,367 miles)

» **Distance from the Sun:** 1.4 billion km (888 million miles)

» **Number of moons:** 62

Rings contain billions of icy fragments.

Gas turns to liquid deep below surface.

Uranus

Uranus is surrounded by at least 11 narrow rings made from dust and rocks. It is tipped over on its side.

FACT FILE

» **Diameter:** 50,724 km (31,506 miles)

» **Distance from the Sun:** 2.9 billion km (1.7 billion miles)

» **Number of moons:** 27

Neptune

This blue planet is named after the ancient Roman god of the Sea. Neptune is really cold as it's 30 times further away from the Sun than the Earth.

FACT FILE

» **Diameter:** 49,244 km (30,599 miles)

» **Distance from the Sun:** 4.5 billion km (2.8 billion miles)

» **Number of moons:** 14

Earth's Moon

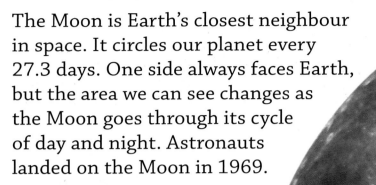

The Moon is Earth's closest neighbour in space. It circles our planet every 27.3 days. One side always faces Earth, but the area we can see changes as the Moon goes through its cycle of day and night. Astronauts landed on the Moon in 1969.

Montes Apenninus range

Mountains
Many of the Moon's mountain ranges are actually the raised edges of huge craters formed from the largest impacts.

Impact craters
There is no air on the Moon to shield it from space rocks hitting its surface. Craters are made when the rocks hit.

Tycho crater

Lunar seas

Sea of Serenity

Long ago, lava from deep impacts in the surface and from volcanoes, flooded the Moon's low-lying areas, before freezing into dark, smooth plains known as seas. The Sea of Serenity was made this way.

! **REALLY?**

The Moon is made of rocks thrown off the Earth when the Earth hit a **huge asteroid**.

Moon landing

Buzz Aldrin's footprint

Apollo 11 landed on the edge of the Sea of Tranquility in 1969. It was the first space mission where astronauts, including Buzz Aldrin, walked on the Moon!

Lunar rover

In 1972, the Apollo 17 astronauts used a special car called the "lunar roving vehicle" to explore the area around their landing site and collect rock samples.

Moons

Most of the planets in the Solar System have a moon or moons of their own. Even asteroids can have a moon. Each moon can vary in shape, size, surface, and atmosphere.

Titan

One of Saturn's moons, Titan, is 50 per cent larger than the Earth's moon. This moon has a thick atmosphere and oily lakes on its surface.

Dactyl

This tiny moon orbits around an asteroid called Ida. It formed when Ida collided with another asteroid. Dactyl is a part of Ida that broke off in the crash.

Ida (an asteroid)

Jupiter

Pluto

Deimos

Mars has two moons. Deimos is the smaller of the two. In Greek, the word Deimos means "terror".

Triton

Neptune has 14 known moons. Triton is the largest. It is bitterly cold and has jets of gas erupting from its surface.

Io

This moon of Jupiter is covered in volcanoes. There are more than 80 major volcanic areas on the surface of Io.

Charon

Pluto has five moons. Charon is the biggest and is more than half the size of Pluto itself!

Neptune

Saturn

Mars

Meteors

Shooting stars or meteors are brief streaks of light across the night sky. They are caused when specks of dust enter Earth's atmosphere, collide with its gases, and heat up. Many meteors arrive in "showers" that are repeated every year.

Meteorites

Space rocks that survive their trip through the atmosphere and hit the ground are called meteorites. Most are chunks of asteroids, broken apart during collisions, but some come from the surface of the Moon or even Mars.

Rocks in space

As well as planets and the Sun, our Solar System is filled with countless smaller objects that have changed little since the birth of the Solar System. They range from country-sized asteroids and city-sized comets to tiny flecks of dust.

Comets

Comets are chunks of ice and rock that mostly orbit at the edge of the Solar System. When a comet comes close to the Sun, some of its ice turns to gas, surrounding it with a fuzzy cloud called a coma, and sometimes a long tail.

Asteroids

Asteroids are rocks left behind from when the Solar System formed. They mostly orbit in an asteroid belt between Mars and Jupiter, but some come closer to Earth. Most are small, shapeless lumps of rock, but the largest asteroid of all, Ceres, has ice on its surface and a very thin atmosphere.

Ida and Dactyl
Ida is a potato-shaped asteroid about 60 kilometres (37 miles) long. It has a tiny moon, called Dactyl, that probably started out as part of Ida before being knocked away in a collision with another asteroid.

Comet NEAT
This comet flew past the Sun in 2003. It's named after the Near Earth Asteroid Tracking (NEAT) project that discovered it. Its long, stretched orbit means it will not return for tens of thousands of years.

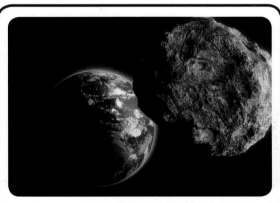

A NEO flies past Earth.

Near-Earth Objects

Some asteroids and comets, called Near-Earth Objects, come close to Earth's orbit through space. There's only a small chance of a collision, but over Earth's long history it's happened many times.

The view from Earth

On a clear night we can see patterns of stars in the sky. These groupings are called constellations. They vary depending on whether we are viewing the sky from above or below the equator, the imaginary line around the middle of Earth. We can also see the Moon, the Milky Way, galaxies, and planets in the night sky.

Milky Way
Our galaxy is a huge, flattened disc of stars, but because our Solar System sits inside this disc, we see many more stars in some directions and far fewer in other directions.

The planet Venus is easy to see as it shines brighter than any star.

Andromeda Galaxy

The Moon's thin crescent is lit by sunlight, while the rest is lit by earthshine.

Glowing star
Venus is called our evening and morning star. It orbits closer to the Sun than Earth, so it always appears close to the Sun in the sky. We can see Venus glowing in the evening or in the early morning.

Brightest galaxy
Most galaxies are too far away to see without a telescope. One huge spiral galaxy two million light years (the distance light travels in a year) away looks like a fuzzy patch in the sky – it's called the Andromeda Galaxy.

Constellations

The stars we see in the night sky from Earth are grouped together in various patterns. These star patterns are known as constellations. There are 88 different constellations. They are named after mythical heroes, animals, and objects.

Northern hemisphere

Southern hemisphere

Northern and Southern stars

Astronomers have divided the night sky into two halves, or hemispheres – that is – the stars seen over the northern half of Earth and those seen over the southern half of Earth.

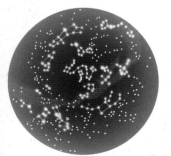

Northern hemisphere

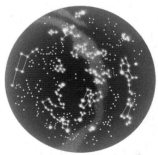

Southern hemisphere

CEPHEUS

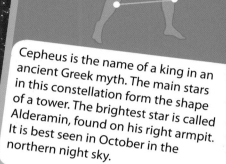

Cepheus is the name of a king in an ancient Greek myth. The main stars in this constellation form the shape of a tower. The brightest star is called Alderamin, found on his right armpit. It is best seen in October in the northern night sky.

PAVO

This southern constellation is shaped like a peacock with its fan-like tail. Alpha Pavonis, the peacock, is a blue-white giant star on the neck of the bird. It is five times as wide as the Sun and shines 2,200 times more brightly.

CASSIOPEIA

Cassiopeia is the name of a queen in an ancient Greek myth. This constellation links five bright stars to form a W-shaped pattern on its side. It can be seen throughout the year in the northern night sky.

URSA MAJOR

Ursa Major, the Great Bear, is a large constellation seen all year round in the northern night sky. Seven stars (joined in red), starting from the tail to the body, form a saucepan shape called the Plough.

CENTAURUS

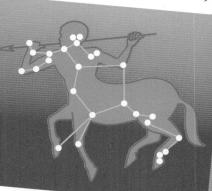

This large southern constellation forms a mythical beast called a centaur – half man, half horse. Alpha Centauri is a group of three stars, forming the brightest star in the front hoof. These are the closest stars to Earth after the Sun.

CRUX

The cross in the southern night sky is the smallest constellation, but is one of the easiest to spot. It is best seen in May. Four main stars create the cross pattern. There is also a bright cluster of stars within the constellation that are called the Jewel Box.

43

Astronomy

Astronomy is the science of studying planets, stars, and other space objects. As we can't visit most of them, astronomers learn about them by collecting information using telescopes.

Newton's reflector

Newton was a British scientist who made amazing discoveries in the 1600s. In 1668, he made a telescope that used a curved mirror to collect light. It made an image that is brighter and more detailed than we could see with our own eyes.

PARKES OBSERVATORY

Many objects that do not shine in visible light still give off invisible radio waves. Radio telescopes, such as Parkes Observatory in Australia, collect these weak rays and turn them into electrical signals.

South Pole Telescope

Many space objects create invisible rays as well as light, but these are mostly blocked by Earth's atmosphere. This telescope collects "microwave" rays that make it through the thin Antarctic air.

Atacama Large Millimeter Array

This radio telescope in Chile uses 66 separate dishes that can be moved around and linked together so they work like a single, much larger telescope.

GREAT CANARY TELESCOPE

This telescope has a 10.4 m (34 ft) mirror that collects two million times more light than a human eye, allowing us to see objects far away. It sits on a mountaintop in the Canary Isles.

FAST

China's Five-hundred-meter Aperture Spherical Telescope is the world's largest radio telescope. It cannot move, but it can look at different parts of the sky.

Meet the expert

We put some questions to Suzanna Randall, a European Southern Observatory (ESO) astronomer who currently works at a large radio telescope, in the Atacama Desert, in Chile. She is about to start training for a trip to the International Space Station (ISS).

Q: We know it is something to do with the Universe, but what is your actual job?

A: As an astronomer, I try to understand the Universe by looking at it through telescopes and then comparing what I see with computer simulations. My research focuses on studying pulsating stars using a technique called asteroseismology. This allows us to look inside stars using their pulsations (changing levels of brightness), and learn more about their internal structure and how they were formed.

Q: What do you do for ESO?

A: ESO builds and operates some of the world's largest telescopes in the Chilean Atacama Desert. In addition to doing my own scientific research, I support ALMA, the Atacama Large Millimetre/Sub-millimetre Array, which is made up of 66 individual antennae, which work together to form the largest radio telescope in the world. My tasks for ALMA include helping other astronomers set up their observations, operating the telescope in Chile, and making sure the data is of good quality.

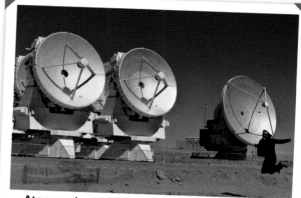

Atacama Large Millimetre/submillimetre Array

Q: What is the "Astronautin" project?

A: It is a private project to send the first female German astronaut into space, to conduct scientific experiments aboard the International Space Station. I was recently selected as one of two trainees for the programme, and hope to fly into space in the next few years.

Q: What excites you most about this opportunity?

A: The part of the training I am most looking forward to are the parabolic flights, where I will get to experience weightlessness for the first time. What excites me most about going into space is

to break that final frontier and go where not many have gone before. That would really be the adventure of a lifetime!

Q: What is a usual work day like for you?

A: A work day for me can range from sitting in my office looking at astronomical data or working a night shift in the desert, to giving presentations at events.

Q: What made you decide to become an astronomer?

A: I became fascinated with space at a young age, reading everything I could get my hands on about the subject and going stargazing in my back garden on clear nights. My dream was always to travel to space, but since that seemed completely out of reach I decided to become an astronomer and study the Universe from afar instead. I feel very lucky that I may now get to do both!

Q: What do you love about the Universe?

A: I love that the size of the Universe is simply mind-boggling!

Space photos

Orbiting high above the atmosphere, the Hubble Space Telescope (HST) gives astronomers on Earth their clearest view of the Universe. Launched in 1990, it is still going strong and providing scientists with information about the way our Universe works.

Aperture door

This shutter can close to protect the mirror and instruments from fierce, direct sunlight.

Maintenance

Astronauts using the US Space Shuttle carried out five missions to repair and upgrade the HST, allowing it to operate for much longer than its planned lifetime of 15 years.

Solar panels

Hubble's "wings" use energy from sunlight to make electricity, which powers its computers and instruments.

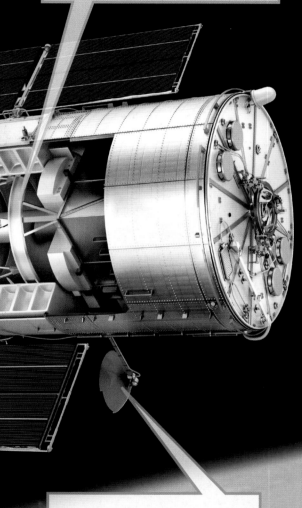

Primary mirror

A curving mirror, 2.4 metres (7.9 ft) wide, collects light from distant objects, and directs it to cameras to record images and information.

Radio dish

The HST sends pictures and other data back to Earth through a special network of satellites.

Amazing images

The HST has taken thousands of amazing space photos, capturing everything from storms on the outer planets to colliding galaxies and the birth of new stars.

V838 Monocerotis

Dying star
After this dying giant star suddenly grew 600 times brighter than normal in 2002, Hubble captured light from its outburst reflecting off nearby gas clouds.

Hubble Ultra-Deep Field

Galaxies
By staring at the same patch of sky for a million seconds, the HST captured faint light from some of the most distant galaxies in the Universe.

Exploring space

Humans have been exploring space since 1957, when the first artificial satellite was launched. Since then, astronauts have reached the Moon, while robot space probes have explored most of the Solar System.

First artificial satellite
Sputnik 1 was launched by Russia on 4 October 1957, and beamed radio signals down to Earth.

Space Shuttle
Between 1981 and 2011, NASA's Space Shuttle carried 355 different people into space.

Discovery

"Buzz" Aldrin

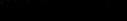
Keck Observatory

Telescopes
The 1990s saw the use of new and more powerful telescopes that can see objects at the edge of the Universe.

Cassini-Huygens near Saturn

Mission to Saturn
From 2004 to 2017, NASA's Cassini probe sent back pictures of the ringed planet Saturn and its moons.

New Horizons

First animal in space
Sputnik 2 carried a dog called Laika into space, but she did not survive the trip.

Laika

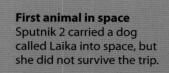

Sputnik 1
This battery-powered satellite was very basic, with four antennae and a radio transmitter.

Yuri Gagarin

Man on the Moon
In 1969, NASA's Apollo 11 mission landed on the Moon carrying astronauts Neil Armstrong, "Buzz" Aldrin, and Michael Collins.

First man in space
In 1961, Russian astronaut Yuri Gagarin spent 108 minutes orbiting Earth on his Vostok 1 spacecraft.

Opportunity
This 1.5 m (5 ft) tall rover has explored Mars since 2004.

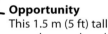

Mars rover
In 2004, NASA landed a pair of wheeled robot explorers, Spirit and Opportunity, on Mars.

International Space Station
Between 1998 and 2011, space agencies worked together to build a huge space station in Earth's orbit.

Rosetta
This space probe started its mission in 2004 and ended in 2016.

Comet 67P

Pluto explorer
In 2015, NASA's New Horizons space probe collected data and took amazing images of Pluto and its moons.

Rosetta (Philae lander)
The European space probe Rosetta entered orbit around comet 67P in 2014, and put a lander called Philae on its surface.

Exoplanets

Planets orbiting around other stars (not our Sun) are called exoplanets. Several thousand have been discovered since the 1990s. Most are very different from Earth, but a few seem to be quite like our planet, and might even be home to living things.

Alien star
The star Kepler-186 is a cool red dwarf much fainter than our Sun.

Another Earth?
Kepler-186f is a planet orbiting in the habitable zone around its star. It could have water on its surface and perhaps even oceans, clouds, and ice caps, like Earth.

Discovering exoplanets

Most exoplanets are too faint to see directly – their dim light is easily drowned out. So astronomers find them by looking for the ways they affect their stars.

51 Pegasi b

First exoplanet
The first exoplanets to be discovered were huge gas giants even bigger than Jupiter. These are big enough to make their stars "wobble" as they go around them.

Habitable zones

A star's habitable zone is the area that is not too hot or too cold for oceans to survive on an exoplanet's surface. Water is necessary for human life to exist, which is why we continue to search for planets that might have water.

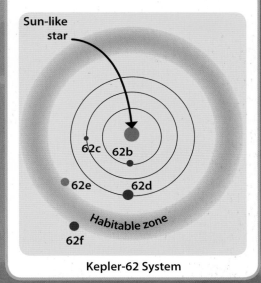

Sun-like star

62c   62b

62e   62d

Habitable zone

62f

Kepler-62 System

Distant neighbour
It would take around 500 years to reach Kepler-186f, even if we could travel at the speed of light, the fastest speed there is.

! WOW!

Astronomers think there could be **60** billion habitable planets in our galaxy!

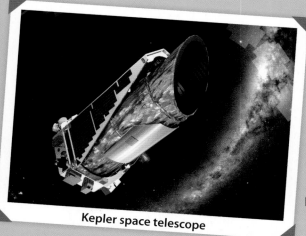

Kepler space telescope

New exoplanets
Space telescopes, such as Kepler find exoplanets by looking for signs that some of a star's light is being blocked by a planet passing in front of it.

Arecibo Observatory, Puerto Rico

Pioneer 10
Robot space probes such as Pioneer 10 will take thousands of years to reach nearby stars, but will keep travelling forever. They carry messages from humanity for anyone who eventually finds them.

Arecibo Observatory
This 305–m (1,000–ft) diameter dish collects radio signals from the distant Universe. Volunteers use computers to look for patterns that might hint at other life being present in the Universe.

Is there life out there?

Some of the biggest questions we have are whether life exists elsewhere in the Universe, and whether we might one day make contact with intelligent aliens. Here are a few attempts astronomers have made to find them.

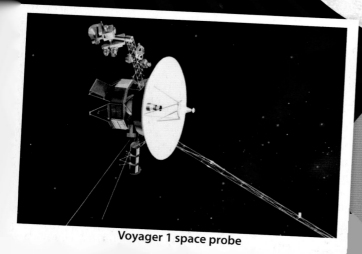
Voyager 1 space probe

Voyager 1
The most distant space probe from Earth, Voyager 1 has now left our Solar System. It carries a golden disc that can recreate sounds and pictures from Earth.

Messages

The search for intelligent aliens mostly involves looking for signs of their activity, such as radio signals, but humans have also sent messages to the stars.

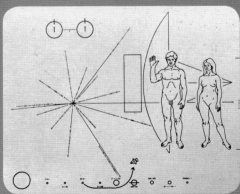

Pioneer 10 space probe

Arecibo message
In 1974, radio signals were sent from the Arecibo radio telescope to a distant cluster of stars called M13. The message included the numbers one to ten, what a human looks like, the Earth's population, and where the Earth sits in the Solar System.

Allen Telescope Array
42 radio dishes scanning the sky in northern California form part of the Search for Extra-Terrestrial Intelligence (SETI) programme. As well as looking for alien signals, they measure radio waves coming from natural cosmic sources.

Radio receivers in the Allen Telescope Array

Pioneer plaque
A plaque fixed to Pioneers 10 and 11 shows two humans and the location of our Solar System.

James Webb Space Telescope

In 2020, NASA's JWST will be launched into space. It will be the biggest telescope in space and it will see the Universe in more detail than ever before, revealing the secrets of planets, the most distant galaxies, and the very first stars.

Massive mirror

The JWST's huge mirror is 6.5 m (21 ft) wide – not far off the biggest Earth-based telescopes. It is made of 18 hexagonal segments that unfold after launch.

An average adult person is 1.8 m (6 ft) tall.

Hubble space telescope mirror is 2.4 m (7.8 ft) wide.

JWST mirror is 6.5 m (21.3 ft) wide.

WHAT'S IN THE PICTURE?

» **1 Sun-facing side** The JWST keeps its underside facing the Sun so the telescope itself is always in the cold and dark.

» **2 Primary mirror** Segments of gold-coated beryllium reflect visible light and infrared rays to the secondary mirror.

» **3 Secondary mirror** This mirror collects light from the primary mirror and bounces it to the tertiary mirror.

» **4 Tertiary mirror** This box-like mirror system directs light to one of several different instruments.

» **5 Science instrument module** Cameras and other devices collect and study the visible and infrared light.

» **6 Solar panels** These panels, in permanent sunlight, make electricity from sunlight to power the telescope.

Sun shield

A high-tech parasol the size of a tennis court protects the telescope in space. It is made from five layers of lightweight material that reflects the Sun's heat and light.

Future missions

New space telescope and robot probes are being launched all the time to help us discover more about different parts of our Universe.

OSIRIS-REx
Launched in 2016, this spaceprobe is on its way to an asteroid called Bennu. It will study Bennu from orbit for 500 days before returning to Earth, hopefully with a sample of material from the asteroid's surface, in 2023.

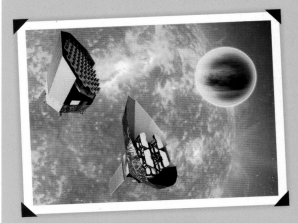

PLAnetary Transits and Oscillations of stars
PLATO is planned for launch in 2026. This space telescope will look for signs of exoplanets around yellow dwarf stars, such as our Sun, red dwarf stars, and subgiant stars.

Universe facts and figures

Our Universe is an amazing place. The facts on these pages may give you some idea of just how amazing it really is.

SPACEWALKS USUALLY LAST BETWEEN 5 AND 8 HOURS.

Astronauts learn what it feels like in space by training **12 m (40 ft) underwater** for **8 hours** at a time!

1,300

Jupiter is so large, it can fit more than 1,300 Earths inside it.

44,000 kg

Scientists estimate that around 44,000 kg (97,000 lbs) of meteorites and space debris lands on Earth every day.

Space is silent because sound cannot travel without air.

On 19 January, 2018, the International Space Station completed a record **7,000 days** orbiting the Earth.

Ptolemy's theory that the **Earth** was the **centre** of the **Universe** was believed to be true until the **16th century**.

In 2007, tiny creatures called tardigrades lived for **10 days** in space outside a Russian unmanned spacecraft.

Studies of lunar rocks brought over by the Apollo missions have revealed that the Moon is **4.51 billion years old!**

100 BILLION TRILLION

is the estimated number of stars in the part of the Universe we can observe.

8½

It took the Space Shuttle only 8½ minutes to travel from the launchpad to low-Earth orbit.

Glossary

Here are the meanings of some words that are useful for you to know when learning about the Universe.

asteroid Small, rocky object that orbits between the planets

asteroid belt Area between Mars and Jupiter where most asteroids orbit

astronaut Any person that goes into space

atmosphere Layer of gases around a planet or moon

binary star Pair of stars that orbit around one another

black hole Object with such strong gravity that light cannot escape it

comet Small, icy object in orbit around a star

condense Decrease in size or volume

constellation Area of the sky containing a pattern of stars

core Hot centre of a planet or star

crater Bowl-shaped hollow in an object's crust, often created by an impact from space

crust Hard outer layer of a rocky planet

debris Material that is left behind after a star or planet has formed

dwarf planet Five objects, including Pluto, are known as dwarf planets, smaller than the main eight planets

Earth, the Our planet, the third main planet from the Sun

exoplanet Planet that orbits a star outside our Solar System

galaxy Huge cloud of stars, gas and dust in space

gravity Force that pulls things towards objects with mass

hemisphere Astronomers have divided the night sky into two halves, or hemispheres – that is – the stars seen over the northern half of Earth and those seen over the southern half of Earth.

Jupiter Fifth main planet from the Sun, and the largest of all the planets in our Solar System

light year Distance light travels in one year, a unit used to measure distances in astronomy

lunar Word meaning "belonging to the Moon"

mass The amount of matter that an object contains

Mars Reddish-coloured, fourth planet from the Sun

Mercury Smallest main planet in our Solar System, and also the closest to the Sun

meteor Shooting star caused by dust entering Earth's atmosphere

meteorite Rock from space that hits a planet's surface

New Horizons space probe

Milky Way Spiral galaxy that contains our Solar System

moon Natural satellite orbiting around a planet or other object

nebula Cloud of gas and dust in space

NEO (Near Earth Object) Asteroid or comet whose orbit brings it close to Earth's

Neptune Eighth and outermost main planet in our Solar System

nova Star that suddenly increases in brightness

orbit Path that one object takes around another thanks to the pull of gravity

parabolic flight Flight simulation that makes someone feel weightless

planet Large object in its own orbit around a star

Pluto Icy dwarf planet orbiting beyond Neptune

protostar Star in the early stages of formation

red dwarf Small, very faint but common type of star

red giant Dying star that is very big and bright

red supergiant Dying monster star

Astronaut on a spacewalk mission

rover Wheeled robot that explores the surface of a planet or a moon

satellite Any object in orbit around another one

Saturn Sixth main planet in the Solar System, famous for its rings

solar Word meaning "belonging to the Sun"

Solar System Region of space dominated by the Sun, and all the objects within it

space Mostly empty region between objects such as planets, stars, and galaxies

spacecraft Vehicle (with or without a crew) that travels through space

spacesuit Clothes that protect an astronaut from exposure to space

spacewalk Any activity that an astronaut does outside of their spacecraft

space probe Robot that explores space and sends information back to Earth

star Huge ball of gas generating heat and light

supernova Brilliant explosion that marks the death of some stars

telescope Device that creates bright, magnified images of distant, faint objects

Universe Whole of space and all the objects within it

Uranus Seventh main planet from the Sun, smaller than Jupiter or Saturn but much bigger than the Earth

Venus Second planet from the Sun

volcano Gap in a planet's crust that erupts hot, molten rock from below

white dwarf Tiny, but still hot and glowing core of a dead star

Index

Acknowledgments

The publisher would like to thank the following people for their assistance: Shalini Agrawal for editorial assistance, Polly Goodman for proofreading, Helen Peters for compiling the index, Anne Damerell for legal assistance, Dan Crisp for illustrations, and Seepiya Sahni for design assistance. The publishers would also like to thank Suzanna Randall for the "Meet the expert" interview.

The publisher would like to thank the following for their kind permission to reproduce their photographs:

(Key: a-above; b-below/bottom; c-center; f-far; l-left; r-right; t-top)

2 Getty Images: SSPL (bc). 3 ESA / Hubble: NASA (bl). NASA. 4 Dreamstime.com: Cao Hai (bl). NASA. 5 NASA and The Hubble Heritage Team (AURA/STScI): NASA, ESA, H. Teplitz and M. Rafelski (IPAC / Caltech), A. Koekemoer (STScI), R. Windhorst (Arizona State University), and Z. Levay (STScI) (tr). NASA: JPL-Caltech (cl). Science Photo Library: Mark Garlick (c). 8-9 NASA: Hubble Heritage Team (cb). 8 NASA: ESA / Hubble (tl); JPL (bl). 9 NASA. 10 NASA: ESA / Herschel / PACS / L. Decin et al (br); JPL-Caltech / ESA, the Hubble Heritage Team (STScI / AURA) and IPHAS (c). 10-11 NASA and The Hubble Heritage Team (AURA/STScI): NASA, ESA, and the Hubble Heritage Team (STScI / AURA)-ESA / Hubble Collaboration (Background). 11 ESO: I. Appenzeller, W. Seifert, O. Stahl (tl). NASA and The Hubble Heritage Team (AURA/STScI): NASA, ESA, and K. Sahu (STScI) (tc). NASA: CXC / NCSU / S.Reynolds et al (bl); X-ray: NASA / CXC / University of Amsterdam / N.Rea et al; Optical: DSS (cl); ESA (bc). 12 NASA and The Hubble Heritage Team (AURA/STScI): NASA, N. Walborn and J. Maíz-Apellániz (Space Telescope Science Institute, Baltimore, MD), R. Barbá (La Plata Observatory, La Plata, Argentina) (tl); NASA, ESA, J. Muzerolle (STScI), E. Furlan (NOAO and Caltech), K. Flaherty (University of Arizona / Steward Observatory), Z. Balog (Max Planck Institute for Astronomy), and R. Gutermuth (University of Massachusetts, Amherst) (cr). 13 NASA and The Hubble Heritage Team (AURA/STScI): NASA, ESA, and A. Feild (STScI) (tl). 14 Dreamstime.com: Levgenii Tryfonov / Trifff (crb). 15 Dreamstime.com: Levgenii Tryfonov / Trifff (clb). 16 NASA: JPL-Caltech / UCLA (cl). 17 Dreamstime.com: Tragoolchitr Jittasaiyapan. 19 NASA: JPL-CalTech (cb). 20 NASA: Hubble Heritage Team, ESA (bl); X-ray: CXC / SAO; Optical: Detlef Hartmann; Infrared: JPL-Caltech (c). 21 ESA / Hubble: NASA (cra). Getty Images: Robert Gendler / Visuals Unlimited, Inc. (br); Stocktrek Images (clb).

NASA: ESA / Hubble (tl). 22-23 NASA: JPL-Caltech (t). 23 Alamy Stock Photo: Heritage Image Partnership Ltd (cb). Getty Images: SSPL (b). NASA and The Hubble Heritage Team (AURA/STScI): NASA, ESA, SSC, CXC, and STScI (cr). Science Photo Library: Chris Butler (tr). 24-25 Dreamstime.com: Levgenii Tryfonov / Trifff. 24 NASA: SDO / AIA / Goddard Space Flight Center (clb). 25 NASA: Johns Hopkins APL / Steve Gribben (tr); SDO / HMI (tl). 26 Dreamstime.com: Levgenii Tryfonov / Trifff (c). 27 NASA: JHUAPL / SwRI (tc). 34 NASA. 34-35 Dreamstime.com: Astrofireball (c). 35 NASA. 36-37 NASA: JPL / University of Arizona (ca). 36 NASA. 37 NASA: JHUAPL / SwRI (cr); JPL (tr, tl). 38 Dreamstime.com: Eraxion (cr). 38-39 NASA. 39 123RF.com: Mopic (crb). NASA: JPL (tr). 40 Dreamstime.com: Zhasmina Ivanova. 41 ESO: Y. Beletsky (l); Babak Tafreshi (r). 42-43 Dreamstime.com: Michal Rojek (Background). 44 Dreamstime.com: Antonio Ribeiro (br). Getty Images: SSPL (bl). 44-45 Science Photo Library: NSF / Steffen Richter / Harvard University (t). 45 Alamy Stock Photo: Blickwinkel (bl); Newscom (tr); Xinhua (br). 46-47 ESO: Hill Media / Astronautin. 46 Suzanna Randall: (cra). 48 NASA. 48-49 NASA. 49 NASA: ESA (cra); ESA / S. Beckwith(STScI) and The HUDF Team (crb). 50 Alamy Stock Photo: Richard Wainscoat (c). Dreamstime.com: Elena Duvernay / Elenaphoto21 (bl). Getty Images: Photo 12 / UIG (br). NASA. 51 123RF.com: Paul Wishart / British Council (ca). Alamy Stock Photo: SPUTNIK (tr). ESA: Rosetta / MPS for OSIRIS Team MPS / UPD / LAM / IAA / SSO / INTA / UPM / DASP / IDA (br). Getty Images: Elena Duvernay / Stocktrek Images (cb). NASA: JPL / Cornell University (cl). 52-53 NASA: Ames / JPL-Caltech / T. Pyle (t). 52 NASA: JPL-Caltech (br). 53 NASA: Ames / JPL-Caltech (bl). 54 Alamy Stock Photo: LOOK Die Bildagentur der Fotografen GmbH (tl). NASA. 55 Alamy Stock Photo: World History Archive (crb). Getty Images: Mark Thiessen (clb). NASA. Science Photo Library: (cr). 56-57 NASA: Northrop Grumman Corporation. 57 Alamy Stock Photo: NASA Image Collection (ca). ESA: (crb). NASA: GSFC (cra). 58 NASA. Science Photo Library: Mark Garlick (bl). 58-59 Dreamstime.com:

Sebastian Kaulitzki / Eraxion (c). 59 NASA. 60 Alamy Stock Photo: Newscom (tl). Getty Images: Photo 12 / UIG (br). 61 NASA. 62 ESO: I. Appenzeller, W. Seifert, O. Stahl (tl). 64 Dreamstime.com: Tedsstudio (tl)

Cover images: Front: Dreamstime.com: Levgenii Tryfonov / Trifff crb; ESA / Hubble: NASA, M. Robberto (Space Telescope Science Institute / ESA) and the Hubble Space Telescope Orion Treasury Project Team tl; Getty Images: Elena Duvernay / Stocktrek Images tr, Alberto Ghizzi Panizza / Science Photo Library bl; NASA: JPL / Cornell University br, X-ray: CXC / SAO; Optical: Detlef Hartmann; Infrared: JPL-Caltech cr; Science Photo Library: Mark Garlick fcra; Back: Dorling Kindersley: Andy Crawford cr; Spine: NASA: JPL cb; Front Flap: Alamy Stock Photo: Richard Wainscoat cb; Dreamstime.com: Astrofireball cr, Eraxion cla / (2), Sebastian Kaulitzki / Eraxion cla; Getty Images: Photo 12 / UIG cla/ (Space probe); NASA: ESA / Rosetta / MPS for OSIRIS Team MPS / UPD / LAM / IAA / SSO / INTA / UPM / DASP / IDA cr/ (2), Hubble Heritage Team, ESA c; Back Flap: Dorling Kindersley: Natural History Museum, London cb; iStockphoto.com: Naumoid tc.

All other images © Dorling Kindersley
For further information see:
www.dkimages.com

My Findout facts:

Careers in Space

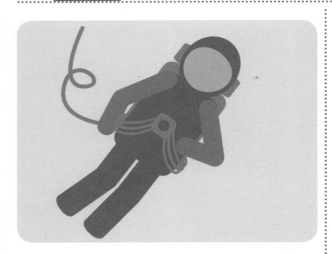

ASTRONAUT

Job description: Astronauts are the people who get to visit space. They work in teams on space missions, they collect data, and conduct experiments in space. They also pilot spacecraft and live on space stations.

PROGRAMMER/ENGINEER

Job description: This role helps to design and make spacecraft, spacesuits, robots, and equipment that is used in space and on the Earth to help with the study of the Universe.

TECHNICIAN

Job description: Technicians test products to be used in the study of space. They also look after and repair spacecraft, including important equipment for space navigation and communication.

ASTROGEOLOGIST

Job description: Astrogeologists help us to understand what makes up planets, moons, and comets. They look at samples and study the surface of a planet to find out about a planet's history.